TROMBONES

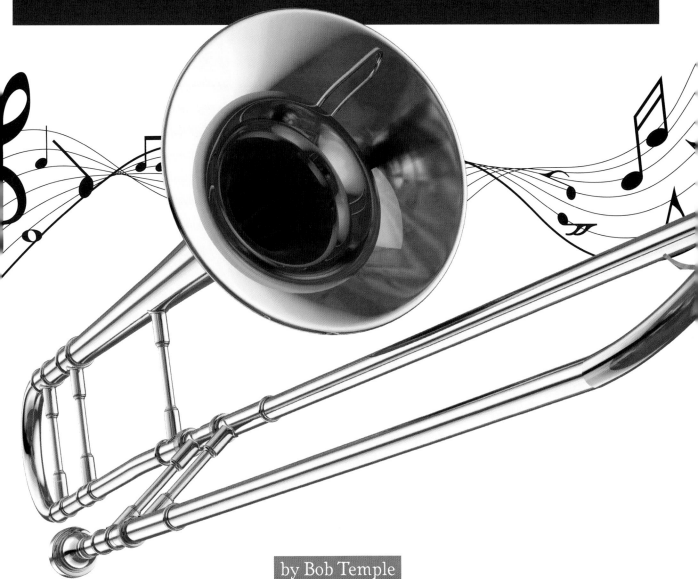

by Bob Temple

Published by The Child's World®
1980 Lookout Drive • Mankato, MN 56003-1705
800-599-READ • www.childsworld.com

Design element: Vector memory/Shutterstock.com
Photo credits: ayzek/Shutterstock.com: cover, 1; Chromakey/Shutterstock.com: 21 (French horn);
furtseff/Shutterstock.com: 7; Horatiu Bota/Shutterstock.com: 21 (flügelhorn and pocket trumpet);
Mark Herreid/Shutterstock.com: 4; Maren Winter/Shutterstock.com: 11; pxl.store/Shutterstock.com:
17; Roman Voloshyn/Shutterstock.com; 18; Sashkin/Shutterstock.com: 21 (bugle); shyshak roman/
Shutterstock.com: 12; the palms/Shutterstock.com: 21 (tuba); Walter Bilotta/Shutterstock.com: 21
(trumpet); wernerimages 2018/Shutterstock.com: 8; Yuri Gurevich/Shutterstock.com: 14;

ISBN: 9781503831858
LCCN: 2018960414

Printed in the United States of America
PA02417

Table *of* Contents

CHAPTER ONE

The Trombone

As you sit along the parade route, you hear the loud, happy sound of a marching band coming down the street. It marches by, playing upbeat music. As the band goes by, you see all kinds of different instruments—flutes, trumpets, drums, and many more.

One kind of instrument looks different from the rest. The people playing these instruments slide something forward and back as they play. What is this strange-looking instrument? It's a trombone!

❮ *This military band has lots of trombones.*

CHAPTER TWO

Brass Instruments

Wind instruments make sound when you blow air through them. **Brass instruments** are a kind of wind instrument made of metal. Most brass instruments have buttons or **valves** you press to change the sound. A trombone doesn't have valves, but it is still a brass instrument. Instead of valves, it has a **slide** to change its sound.

A player uses his or her right hand to move the slide. ❯

CHAPTER THREE

Where Did Trombones Come From?

Hundreds of years ago, there was no such thing as a trombone. Musicians played trumpets instead. People learned that they could change the trumpet's sound by adding more tubing. In the 1400s, they added a U-shaped piece of tubing that could slide in and out of the rest of the instrument.

❮ *Trombones might look heavy, but they're really fairly light.*

Sliding the instrument's tube in and out changed the sound, even without valves. At first this instrument was called the "sackbut." Over time, it became known as the trombone.

The sackbut started changing into the modern trombone in the 1750s.

Players use a special grease on the slide to make it glide easily. ❯

CHAPTER FOUR

The Trombone's Shape

The trombone is a long, curved instrument. It looks a little like a long, skinny letter S bent in half. You hold the slide gently in your right hand. You hold the other half of the S over your left shoulder. Most players point the slide down or slightly up so they don't hit other people in the head with it!

A person who plays a trombone is called a trombonist.

❮ *You can see how this man holds his trombone.*

13

CHAPTER FIVE

Parts of a Trombone

A trombone is a long, hollow tube made of a metal called brass. You blow air into a small, cup-shaped opening called a **mouthpiece**. The air moves through the tube-like body and the movable slide. At the other end of the body is the large opening, or **bell**, where the sound comes out.

> The word "trombone" comes from tromba, *the Italian word for "large trumpet."*

❮ *The mouthpiece goes up above your top lip.*

Sometimes trombone players hold a separate piece called a **mute** in front of the bell. The mute blocks some of the air and sound that come out of the trombone. The mute makes the trombone sound softer and quieter.

Players can change a trombone's sound by moving the mute as they play.

Mutes like these are often made of cardboard. ❯

CHAPTER SIX

How Do You Play a Trombone?

To play the trombone, you press your lips together and hold them against the mouthpiece. Then you blow air into the mouthpiece. As you blow, you make your lips buzz or **vibrate**. Your vibrating lips create sound. You move the slide in and out to play different notes.

Glenn Miller, Tommy Dorsey, and Trombone Shorty are all famous trombone players.

❮ *You can see how this woman uses her lips to push air through the mouthpiece.*

19

CHAPTER SEVEN

Types of Trombone Music

Early trombones made lower, softer sounds than those used today. People played them in churches and in the courts of kings and queens. Over time, the trombone's tubing was made wider, and the sound became livelier. Trombones began to be used by military bands and by orchestras in opera houses.

Today, they are used in all types of bands, including marching bands and jazz bands. Would you like to play the trombone?

Other Brass Instruments

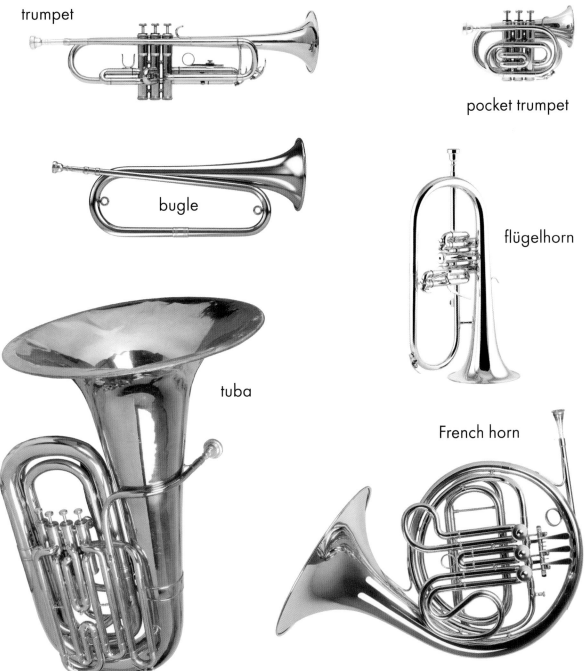

trumpet

pocket trumpet

bugle

flügelhorn

tuba

French horn

Glossary

bell (BELL) The bell is the wide end of a brass instrument, where the sound comes out. Trombones have a bell.

brass instruments (BRASS IN-struh-ments) Brass instruments are made of metal and make sounds when you blow air through them. Trombones are one kind of brass instrument.

mouthpiece (MOWTH-peece) The mouthpiece is the part of an instrument where you place your mouth to play. Trombones have a cup-shaped mouthpiece.

mute (MYOOT) A mute is an object a trombonist puts in the bell to change the instrument's sound.

slide (SLIDE) On a trombone, the slide is the part of the body that moves in and out. The slide changes the length of the trombone's body and the sound it produces.

valves (VALVZ) Most brass instruments have valves, which are buttons you push to change the sound. Trombones have a slide instead of valves.

vibrate (VY-brayt) When something vibrates, it moves back and forth very quickly. To play a trombone, you make your lips vibrate as you blow into the mouthpiece.

wind instruments (WIND IN-struh-ments) Wind instruments make sound when you blow air through them. Trombones are one kind of wind instrument.

To Learn More

IN THE LIBRARY

Andrews, Troy. *Trombone Shorty*. New York, NY: Abrams Books for Young Readers, 2017.

Nunn, Daniel. *Brass.* Chicago, IL: Heinemann Library, 2012.

Russell-Brown, Katheryn and Frank Morrison. *Little Melba and Her Big Trombone.* New York, NY: Lee & Low Books, 2014.

ON THE WEB

Visit our website for links about trombones:

childsworld.com/links

Note to Parents, Teachers, and Librarians: We routinely verify our Web links to make sure they are safe and active sites. So encourage your readers to check them out!

Index

About the Author

Bob Temple is the author of dozens of nonfiction books for children and young adults. He is also an award-winning journalist. Bob enjoys traveling, playing golf, and spending time with his wife and three adult children. Bob lives in Minnesota.